Hey, I'm Here Too!

A Book for Tween/Teen Siblings of a Young Person With Emotional Issues

by Pat Harvey LCSW-C and David Fialkoff

Cover and interior design by David Fialkoff

"Selfie" illustrations by Amy Salsbury
(using Shutterstock images)

Dedicated:

To KW

Who inspired my work with siblings

To CPZ

*Who inspired this story and whose courage and sensitivity
continue to inspire me*

To all of the siblings of kids who have emotional issues

Because you and your feelings really do matter

-PH

To every young person struggling with these issues

-DF

Siblings. You know, brothers, sisters, half-brothers, stepsisters, etc. Most kids have at least one. Some kids have a sibling whom they are close to and maybe even consider their best friend. Other kids may have siblings they fight with. You may have a sibling whom you love sometimes and fight with at other times. Some kids have siblings who may have a physical disability or an illness that requires lots of care. And some kids have siblings whose problems may not be so noticeable to others although you see how much they bother you and your parents. These siblings may have emotions that are so intense that they cause them to behave in unsafe, aggressive, destructive, or abusive ways. Other kids have siblings who are so sad that they may hurt themselves. Kids who have siblings that have emotional problems often find themselves confused by the behavior of siblings who may seem to have it all together at times and act "out of control" at other times. These kids may have many different feelings about their sibling including being angry, sad, protective, and even jealous because their sibling seems to "get away with things" and is treated differently. Kids who have siblings who have emotional problems may feel invisible because of all the time and attention their sibling needs. They may not want to upset their parents and they may not feel that their needs or problems are important enough to talk about.

If you are a kid whose sibling has intense emotions that are causing problems at home, it might help you to know that you are not alone. You might like to know that your feelings, all of them, are real and understandable and that your needs are important too. You might like to know that others care. Sometimes sharing with someone else can help.

March 3 7:14 PM

Whassup?

Hey. It's Sherry.

Nothing. What's up with u Kev?

My sister is at it again

She knocked over something in the living room. I think it was the big lamp. I heard a crash

Ugh

OMG. I hope it wasn't the TV

OMG! It better not have been the TV. Let me go sneak a peek

Whew. Just the lamp. But it still sucks. She makes me so mad when she breaks stuff.

You OK?

Yeah, I guess. Sometimes I feel like I'm trapped. Like in a cage, y'know. Like right now, I'm hungry but I don't want to go down to the kitchen cause she's still yelling.

That's so unfair

Totally. What's up at your house?

Everything's ok

What about your brother? Is he... you know?

Yeah. He's cutting again. I found a razor blade in the bathroom trash

Gross. I mean, sorry to hear about that.

It's no biggie. gtg

5

Sometimes kids feel really scared when a sibling is behaving violently in the house. It is hard to know just what to do. Some kids hide out. Others listen to music. Some kids try to dismiss these concerns as if they are not important. Other kids don't know what to do when they find a sibling self-harming or doing drugs. They don't know what to tell their parents. Do they keep their sibling's confidence or do they tell so their sibling can get help? What happens if the behavior is that your sibling is not eating and every meal is a war zone? What happens if your sibling is so depressed that he/she never leaves his/her room and you feel as though you do not have a sibling at all. These feelings of confusion and anger and fear continue and sometimes feel like they will never end. And so do the thoughts that you and your feelings are not important. Some kids try to share their feelings with someone who might understand. It is important to know that YOUR feelings do matter.

March 7 8:05 PM

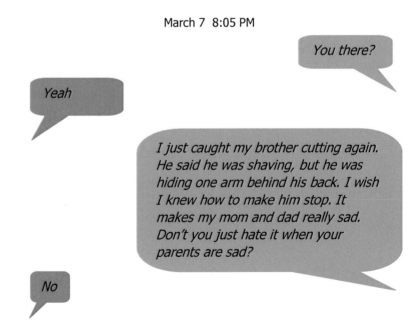

You there?

Yeah

I just caught my brother cutting again. He said he was shaving, but he was hiding one arm behind his back. I wish I knew how to make him stop. It makes my mom and dad really sad. Don't you just hate it when your parents are sad?

No

Why should I?
They don't care
about me.

You don't?
Why not?

Why do you say
that?

I'm the invisible kid. I was in a variety
show at school. I didn't even tell my folks
about it because it was the same night as
you-know-who's therapy appt.

That sucks. That must have
made you feel so sad

I guess. What makes me really angry is
when my sister says mean things to me
and my parents don't do anything to stop
her. It's like they don't even care.

OMG. That sounds awful.
I don't know how I would
feel if my brother did that
to me

Yea, she insults me so much and screams so loud. It's almost scary. I'm really getting tired of her abuse

Sorry

I wish my parents could get her to stop doing that to me or at least defend me. When I complain about it, they just tell me to ignore it. Like I could do that.... They seem so useless.

Sometimes when my parents DO get angry at my brother, he gets so upset that he threatens to hurt himself. Then my parents back off. It's almost like they're scared of him

I know what you mean. My parents just don't know what to do. It's like an alien is living with all of us and we just don't know how to live with her

Don't you wish you could make your family happy somehow so that everyone got along and felt better?

Sometimes I wish I could figure out how to make MYSELF feel better. Sometimes I am so angry I could scream and other times I feel so sad. Sometimes I feel like giving up. I think the only answer would be if I could fly far away and never come back

Yeah, me too. Sometimes.

I do feel better when I talk to you. I don't feel so alone.

Yeah. same here. Gotta go

OK bye

Sometimes life becomes really overwhelming for kids whose siblings have problems and their own lives begin to suffer.

March 9 9:30 PM

They have enough problems already. My mom always says she's "overwhelmed." And my dad sighs all the time. It doesn't matter anyway. One semester I got straight A's and they just said "Way to go." It's like they didn't want to feel too proud of me. Like that would be disloyal to my brother or something

Yeah. I hate that. I want them to feel proud of me sometimes. And I hate when they complain about her when I'm around. It's not my fault. It's not my problem. What do they want me to feel guilty or something?

Don't you?

A little

Me too. I feel bad when I'm having fun and then I think about my brother and his problems and how he never has fun

Yea, me too. Even good times aren't so good. It sux. It sux when they ask me questions about her, like they want me to spy on her for them

My parents do that too. They expect me to tell them everything and I am so tired of it always being about him. They seem to want me to be helpful and perfect

Like we don't feel bad enuf already

Yeah. I feel bad, ok? Bad, mad, and sad. But just because I don't have problems like him, they don't pay attention

14

Eventually all of those confusing, angry, and sad feelings may begin to make it harder for you to enjoy your friends and your activities. Even your schoolwork may suffer. You may feel alone and believe that others will not understand you or that there is something wrong with you. And yet, the feelings may continue to be overwhelming and you may feel the need to get someone to listen and help you. Even though you may feel embarrassed or disloyal talking about what is happening in your family or telling someone how you feel, sometimes it may feel like someone just HAS TO listen.

I wish there was another way. I wish I knew what else I could do. I don't want to act like him.

Yeah. You won't believe what happened. My parents found drugs in my sister's room

What!? What did they do?

They called the cops again

For real? What a bummer!

Yep. I hate when they do that. It's so embarrassing. All the neighbors see

I would be so scared. R U?

Am I what?

Scared?

A little. Usually the police just calm everybody down and leave. I hope they don't this time. I hope this time they take her away. FOREVER

Go and see what's going on

I don't want to. I'd rather stay here talking to you where I feel safe. So I can forget a little

It's nice that we have each other, right? Someone who understands? I'm glad we met at camp

Me too. I'm glad you told me about your brother so I could tell you about my sister. I never told anyone else. It was such a relief to be able to tell someone

I never told anyone either. Lately, though, I am thinking about talking about it with Mr. Lee, my school counselor

> Why would you want to do that? It would just make it worse.

> U think?

> Yeah. Nobody gets it unless they live it. He would just defend your parents and tell you that you have to understand.

> I don't know. Maybe. Sometimes I feel like I am going to burst and I need to tell someone how I feel

> I'm not sure he would get it. Cops are leaving. I better go find out what's going on. I feel so angry at everyone right now...except you.

> I know. I get it. I'll think about what you said. Bye

It may feel hard to reach out and trust an adult. It may feel so hard to trust anyone with your thoughts and feelings, especially when they are so confused and painful. It is hard to believe that anyone would understand. It might feel hopeless, like it cannot get better. And then there is the worry that others might dismiss your feelings or think that you are exaggerating the problem. Maybe the other person will think that YOU are crazy or insensitive. You may worry that others will judge you or your family, and you don't want to betray your family.

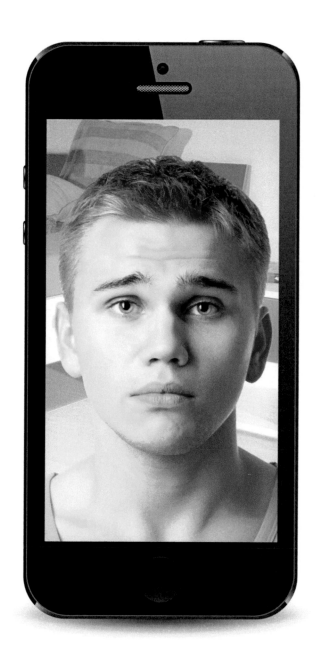

March 12   10:00PM

I did it.

Did what?

I spoke to my guidance counselor.

You did! WOW! What happened?

At first he didn't understand. He asked me questions and it was hard for me to answer them. I was so embarrassed. When I told him how sad I felt, he seemed to get it though. He told me he was sorry I was so sad. He asked what he could do to help.

Did it make you feel better?

A little. It helped that he understood and didn't think that I was exaggerating.

I can't imagine my guidance counselor caring enough to listen.

Well, Mr Lee listened to me. And then he began to explain to me that my brother probably has problems that make him feel things more, like, strongly.

It sounds like he was making excuses for your brother, just like everyone does.

Yeah, it felt like that to me at first. Then I kept listening and he explained that even tho my brother's feelings might not be his fault, he still had to change his behavior so that he was safer and healthier.

I never thought about it like that. What else did he say?

He said that he understood my confusion and my anger. And he also thought that if I understood my brother a little, I might feel better.

See I told you that everyone wants to protect your brother and nobody really cares about you.

21

Sometimes it feels like that. But this time I felt like Mr. Lee got it. He explained my brother's problems to me, and I did feel a little better. Less angry. He also told me to try to find ways to make myself feel better, like listen to music or play video games. Or do something to take my mind off my brother

WOW. It would be great to feel less angry. I would love not to have to listen to all the stuff that goes on

And he told me to talk to my parents.

Are you going to?

I don't know. I don't want to burden them anymore. And I am still afraid that they won't understand.

I know how you feel. I can't imagine actually talking to my parents about this. I don't think they will get it. I'm scared they will get angry at me. What are you going to do?

Not sure. Gonna talk to Mr. Lee again. He said he will help me talk to my parents, even meet them with me if I want. I don't know what to do. Sooooooo confused.

When you are so angry at your sibling and the difficulties he/she is causing in your family, you might not think about ways to soothe, distract, or just enjoy yourself. You may be so caught up in your sibling's behaviors that you forget to do things that you like doing. And yet, you do have to take care of yourself and make sure you are doing things that are fun and that distract you, at least for a little while, from the pain in your family. It is OK for you to take care of yourself and enjoy yourself.

When you see the chaos and pain that your sibling seems to be causing your family, it may be hard to think about the pain he/she may be feeling that may be causing the problems you see. Some people call this "emotional dysregulation," which means your brother's or sister's brain is very sensitive to emotional situations. Your sibling may seem to explode over the littlest thing. Sometimes your brother or sister can seem so "normal" and other times so "crazy." It is really very confusing for everyone and painful for everyone as well. Your sibling does not really want to behave the way he/she does and still does need to learn ways to handle his/her emotions in less destructive ways. Just like you want someone to understand your feelings, so your sibling wants someone to understand and acknowledge the pain he/she is in. Sometimes everyone in the family has to learn how to understand and accept one another. And sometimes, even though it doesn't seem fair that you have to tell them, you may have to remind your parents that you need them too.

March 30 6:10PM

Mom, I need to talk to you.

What's the problem?

I don't know how to start. I'm afraid you'll be mad at me.

Why would you think that? You know you can talk to me. We can always talk about things.

Yes but you always seem so sad these days and it's about Jay. I don't want to make you feel worse

Yes, I'm sad about your brother. I can still listen to you. What happened?

Nothing different happened. It's just...I get so angry at him sometimes and I just...I feel like the family is falling apart. Sometimes I feel so miserable.

I knew something was wrong. I just didn't know what to say to you. And I've been so distracted by your brother's problems.

I don't want to make you feel worse, Mom, but... Sometimes I feel like he gets all of your and Dad's attention. Because of the way he acts. Now I feel bad for telling you. Never mind. I just wanted you to know that I need you too.

I'm glad you told me. You are important too and I don't want either of us to forget that. So please try not to feel guilty about talking to me

One more thing, Mom?

Yes?

Sometimes I want to help him and I don't know what to do.

I know you want to help. It's not your responsibility though. You have to live your own life and I have to make sure you can, even if I forget sometimes.

What about if I know he has hurt himself? I don't want to get him in trouble but I don't want him to die

I know you're scared and you don't always know what to do. If you know something, tell someone. I don't want you to have to carry this burden by yourself.

I think I can do that. Thanks for getting it, Mom.

Let's talk more at home or maybe go out together. OK?

That sounds great Mom.

Sherry took the chance of telling her Mom how she felt and her Mom seemed to understand. She acknowledged her feelings and did not dismiss them. They have to continue the conversation so that Sherry can continue to feel support. She was relieved to finally share this with her mother.

March 30 9:15

> I did it. I texted my Mom about how I feel about my brother.

You did?!And?

> I told her how awful I feel. She was cool. She told me she thinks I'm important too.

No way! Wow

> Yeah! I couldn't deal with it myself anymore. I texted her so I didn't have to see her face. We're gonna talk some more tonight when she gets home.

Let me know how it goes. I dunno. Maybe I'll talk to my Dad tonite.

My Mom said she understood and we needed to talk more. She even said we should talk more often. You should do it! Talk to your Dad

I can't believe she didn't get mad. Gotta work up my courage. And I really don't think he would have time for me anyway.

You know, he might. You're not afraid of him, r u?

No. I just don't think he'll get it.

C'mon. You have to start somewhere. Someone has to take the first step. Might as well be you. Do it. Talk to him.

This is really different. I'm not sure how I feel about what you're saying. You are so brave. I wish I could be like you. I'll see what I can do. Thx for being there

You have to be yourself and figure this out for yourself. Just know that you are not alone. I'm here for you

I'm here for you too

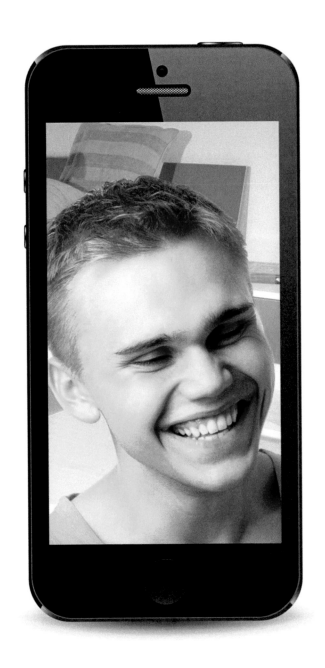

The story now is about Kevin and Sherry and not their siblings. They are no longer invisible, not to themselves, not to each other, and not to their parents. There may still be violence and self-harm and anger and confusion in their homes and, unfortunately, in their lives. And yet, Sherry and Kevin are beginning to take some control over their lives, finding the courage to share their feelings, finding ways to take care of themselves and recognizing that they can live their lives despite the turmoil and sadness in their family. They are on their way to a better place.

You, too, can rewrite your story and make it about you. You can talk to a friend, or an adult at school (like a teacher or coach), or a relative (like an aunt or uncle), or a family friend, or you might talk to a parent. Not every parent will understand or have the energy or ability to help. Other parents might totally get it and do whatever they can to be there for you and meet your needs. The important thing is finding someone that you trust who will listen and who will accept your feelings and understand them. You ARE important too. Try to begin making small changes, as Sherry did when she spoke to her counselor and mother. Do things that help YOU feel good. Make sure that people know that you are here too. You may be surprised that your life can feel a little bit better if you do.

Kids/Teens: This book was written to provide support for you and your feelings as you figure out how to live your life when your sibling's emotional issues seem to dominate your family and intrude on your life. It is understandable that you sometimes feel like nobody "gets it" and you don't know whom you can trust.

The following pages provide information and resources for your parents and other adults in your life so that they can begin to know how to respond in a more helpful and effective way to both your sibling and to you. We ask that you share this book and this information with them so that they can appreciate your needs and feelings and so that they can figure out how to navigate their own emotions and family life in a way that is healthier for all of you. Information can sometimes transform situations and it is our hope that this information and these resources will help bring about changes in your family so that everyone can feel a little bit better and get their needs met in healthy ways.

Resources for Parents and Other Concerned Adults

Websites

NEA-BPD (National Education Alliance for Borderline Personality Disorder)

www.borderlinepersonalitydisorder.com

Provides resources and information about disorders of emotion dysregulation and about dialectical behavior therapy (DBT), as well as information about family support programs

Annenberg Foundation Trust at Sunnylands

www.sunnylands.org

Provides information about the Adolescent Mental Health Initiative, which publishes books for and about teens who have mental health challenges

Pat Harvey LCSW-C

www.patharveymsw.com

Provides information about DBT, and resources for parents and siblings as well as additional resources for family members

PDAN (Personality Disorder Awareness Network)

www.PDAN.org

www.facebook.com/PDAN

Information and resources about personality disorders

BPChildren

www.BPChildren.org.

Information, resources, mood charts, and games for kids who have emotion dysregulation

Unhooked Books

www.unhookedbooks.com

An online bookstore that specializes in books related to families in which there is emotion dysregulation and books related to resolving family conflict

Books

Loving Someone with Borderline Personality Disorder by Shari Manning

Addresses the difficulties of having a family member who has emotion dysregulation while providing helpful ways to manage these difficulties and respond effectively to the family member

Acquainted with the Night by Paul Raeburn

A memoir about how a parent feels and responds when a child has emotional difficulties

Stop Walking on Eggshells and **The Stop Walking on Eggshells Workbook** by Paul Mason and Randi Kreger

Provides support and guidance for family members about how to respond to the behaviors and emotions of a loved one who has emotion dysregulation

Will's Choice by Gail Griffith

A memoir written by a mother about her son's suicide attempt and the ways in which the family sought out the most effective treatment and responses for him

Parenting a Child Who Has Intense Emotions by Pat Harvey and Jeanine Penzo

Provides support, insights, and practical advice for parents of kids who have intense emotions and provides information about how to respond to siblings

The Normal One: Life with a Difficult or Damaged Sibling by Jeanne Safer

In the words of the author's website, this book "takes us into the hidden world of problem siblings and explores the far-reaching effects on the lives of those who are considered the 'normal ones.'"

My Sister's Keeper: Learning to Cope with a Sibling's Mental Illness by Margaret Moorman

A memoir written by a sister that offers insights into the feelings and impact on siblings of individuals with emotion dysregulation/mental illness

Mad House: Growing Up in the Shadow of Mentally Ill Siblings by Clea Simon

A memoir written by the sibling of two children with mental illness about the long-lasting impact on her life and how she moved forward with her life